This J(

Published By Malak

Write Your Unlimited Ideas

Made in the USA
Columbia, SC
07 December 2022

72950904R00074